PAUSING

In the

PASSING PLACES

PAUSING
In the
PASSING PLACES

Alice Scott-Ferguson

CLADACH
Publishing

Pausing In the Passing Places: Poems
Alice Scott-Ferguson
Copyright © 2018

An AGATES Book of Poetry

Published by CLADACH Publishing
PO Box 336144 Greeley, CO 80633
http://cladach.com

Cover art and interior art Copyright © Amy Whitehouse.
Learn more about "Amy Whitehouse Fine Art":
http://AmyWhitehousePaintings.com.

Author photo by Grant Ferguson

ISBN 9781945099083

Printed in the United States of America

To the memory of
my beautiful, brilliant little brother,
Johnnie.
The blood is strong.
The love is stronger.

CONTENTS

INTRODUCTION

I grew up with philosophy, poetry and music. My earliest and fondest memories of childhood are of listening to my mother singing with the voice of a songbird as she accompanied herself on the little pump organ in our living room; of my father reciting poetry from memory, including the 119th Psalm and Tam o' Shanter from the work of his favorite poet, the Scottish bard, Robert Burns; of my brother playing endlessly, and seemingly effortlessly, on his guitar. Our table conversations were loud, lively and searching; the meaning of life, legend and the ways of nature were all up for examination, then were woven with wonder into the tapestry of a strong faith, which became the resting place for all our speculation. We are Celts and thus prone to melancholy, though in my family, winsome wit won over the morbidity of that particular proclivity.

But my parents were not from the nobility, elite or formally educated in a land of deep class divides. They were people of the land and sea in the farthest reaches of the United Kingdom, the Shetland Islands, where the sun never sets in summer and the aurora borealis dances in the long, dark winter skies. It was in that setting I began to express who I was. I would fill pages of paper with my girlie stories and made the prophetic announcement, when very young, that I would publish my first book at aged sixty. And that is exactly what happened!

Now, many years and many miles away from those humble beginnings, three books and innumerable articles later, you now hold this book of poetry in your hands. The title is inspired by the passing places along the narrow, one-lane roads that weave through the moors and the mountains of my native land. As drivers have to pull off the road to let oncoming traffic pass, so in life we often need to do so figuratively: pause, reflect, assess and tuck into a place of safety from the dangers, dreads and distractions.

It is my hope that many of these poems will echo in your heart; that you will identify with their pathos and pain and know you are not alone. I hope you will see the humor in the commonplace and the sacred in everything. My highest hope is that I may have contributed something to interpreting the enigmas and the wonders of this precious planet we call our temporary home. I trust that I have honored bewilderment, brokenness and beauty in such a way that would fulfill the dream of Rainer Maria Rilke, who wrote: "Our task is to stamp this provisional, perishing earth into ourselves so deeply, so painfully and passionately, that its being may rise again, 'invisibly,' in us."

May you be inspired to be the poet of your own precious life from your unique, God-given voice and vantage point!

NATURE

Autumn Observation

Dead leaves
what do you do
what do you give to the ground
where I've found you
packed in profusion
dank and fetid
filling the earth with the fruit of your death?

Beauty shed
dead
forgotten
feeding new life at the end

Montana Gold

Such a silence settles in the fall
   when fields are spent,
   awash in golden glow
   and rolling landscapes rest
   from summer's work.
Through the quietude
   you can almost hear
   a sigh in the stubble—
Relieved of their load of grain
   fields commune together
   in the satisfaction
   of work well done.
A hint of fetid fragrance
   drifts in the stillness.
First fresh snow falling
   on the distant mountains,
   the seal of the season
In rural Montana now.

Crawly Critter

Why does a centipede
  need
    so many pairs of feet?
Would not two do
  even three or four?
But no more!

Today

The scent of orange blossom...i can smell
The sound of cactus wren's exultant nesting...i can hear
The soft cold of my doggies' noses...i can feel
The bliss of the sweet sauvignon grape...i can taste
The opening orchids in their purple glory...i can see

We only ever have TODAY

On Killing Caterpillars

Fat and squirmy
Slow and curving
Caterpillars made me freeze
  in primal terror.

Then I would squelch them
  in their tedious trails
  without compunction
  with satisfaction,

Till one day I heard:

'That caterpillar
  will never float
  and soar in the sky,
  that ugly lumbering life
  never become a butterfly!'

Tears still well in sorrow
  at my lack of love
  and absence of pity.

Without the laborious
  crawling close to the ground
  there'd be no exquisite colors
  flying, catching the kiss of the sun.

The slow and the unlovely among us
  will one day fly in resplendent colors.

Capturing Colorado

The smell of the pines after the rain
First snowflake melting on my tongue
First Pasque flower to show
After the winter is gone…
Though never quite gone in the high country

Snowstorm on the Fourth of July
Riotous sunsets over the distant and enduring mountains
The dazzling and divine décor of gold in the fall
Lying in an aspen grove, gazing into endless blue above
Smelling the starting decay of the fallen leaves under me

My marvelous meadow with its plenitude of wildflowers
The colors of every rainbow arcing over the horizon
After winter's mantle they were waiting
Surprising me now, yet I was waiting too

A mile high piece of land
Pointing far into the sky
Piercing my soul
Sealing my soul
Searing my soul
With its boldness, bigness and beauty

The Sights of the Sea

Blue on the bright days
  reflecting the sky
Gray on the dull days
  promising storm

Still and silent
  reflecting the shoreline
Roaring and cresting
  at the behest of the wind

Dotted with small boats
  plying their trade
Dipping with seabirds
  diving for fish

Lapping waves
  on the pristine sand
Laughing and sparkling
  in the summer sun

Morphing now
  in my memory as me
Flowing in my veins
  the forever sea

Birds of Being

Larks soar and sing
  high in the sky
  over an open grave

The Lonely Curlew
  cries from the heather hills
  missing the familiar footsteps

The Mourning Doves
  sound like wails of wanting
  from the broken hearts

The Mocking Birds
  serenade in the sycamore tree
  celebrating the life that was

Lunar Light

Sister of the sun
ruler of the dark
your alchemy's just right
when lovers melt
under your spell of night
by a shore
where waves break,
whose timing, distance, delivery,
in their predictability,
you take credit for—
trusted by mariners in
calculating their voyages

You tease us
with partial glimpses
until your full face
is unveiled, and your cold
serene beauty bathes the earth

Making magical shadows of
eerie, other worldly breath,
we serenade you,
shining sentinel of velvet sky
studded with myriad companions,
constellations of stars

We are part of it all
though, looking up,
we feel so small

The Aurora Borealis

Plasma particles burst
  from the boiling bosom of the sun
  on its faithful circuit of Earth.

Distorted and twisted magnetic fields
  appear, to our delight,
  as ribbons of the finest silk
  swirling in the northern skies—
  pinks and reds, blues, violets, green—
  dancing randomly in abandoned wild
  with crackling, crossing, swishing sounds.
Merry dancers I called them as a child.

The aurora is exhibit number one
  that ecstasy abounds
  at the Pole,
  in the whole.

The Silence of Spring

Without a sound, you see the
   greening first on the ground
Fruit trees' eager little nubs
   burst, pop flowers into bloom
They in a chorus of silence
   open with face to the sun
Pale and pink, parchment thin,
   brief delight, a riot of quietude
Silently, blossoms shrivel,
   carpeting the green below
Then lavish canopies of leaves
   as trees now fill out all, to
Wait, create the fruit of fall

THE GOD WHO IS

After Visiting an Alzheimer's Unit

Christ doesn't stay in the chapel.
He lives in the lady lost in the fog,
　diapered and demented.
He chooses to live in a frail form,
　not temples made with hands.
His hands shaped her, His eyes watched
　that lovely form lose shape,
　that amazing mind become
　a tangled web of crossed lines.
Mistake?

You will not leave the lady,
　she who leaves the chapel.
You are in her to the end
　till you fly away together—
Free, unfettered forever.

Who Am I?

I AM…
A limitless edition
No partition
No separation
No daylight between
   the Divine and me

I AM…
United
No selvedge edge
Smoothly,
Seamlessly one
   with Triune God

I AM…
Connected
Created
A part of the whole
An irreplaceable unit
   in the Creator's purview

I AM…
Your sister
Your friend
Your enemy
From One Womb birthed
   from a Force Field of Love

When Is Now

When will I see
   the mutuality tree
   in full, flourishing bloom?

When will I see
   our male counterparts
   cease their pruning,
   let the tree bear fruit?

When will I hear
   less of the tree in the garden
   and women's deception
   and more of the epiphany
   of exception—
   that God is both male and female
   that nothing less showcases His character
   and anything less is a caricature

When will I hear
   from every tongue and tribe,
   that when God put on flesh
   He took the axe to the old tree
   when He became one of us
   when he rose from His Tree
   and demolished gender differences

When will I hear
   every pulpit proclaim:
All humanity is one

The tree is full of unbridled blooms
   the fruit nourishing and sweet
   foliage protecting and covering
   all the fig leaf never could

Thanks be to our mother father God
The When is the eternal Now

An Either/Or World

It bore a fruit with two parts to the whole,
  the Tree of the Knowledge of Good and Evil—
Partaking of that tempting fruit
  mankind became moral arbiter of his life, alone
And nothing has ever been quite the same

The progeny of those far-flung forefathers
  carry the self-same DNA—
Our world and every system in it
  posits on the premise of only good and bad
So an either/or world continues to this day

The cause of death that ensued from the eating—
  dualistic thought, its name—
  now trumped by transcendence,
  the fruit of another tree
The tree of Life, it is not the same

Its leaves and fruit bring healing
  from consequences of that fateful fall
Transcendent thought is the third way—
  seeing all from a higher plane, hearing the call
  of so much more than either/or

Hell

Well, it is not fire
  but it is dire enough
  without the flames
The torment of regret, remorse, loss
The searing sense of separation,
Fearing as in the Garden
Where He came to seal the split
  though without fire
We are burning with shame
Naked and vulnerable and so afraid
Covered with scant fig leaves
So inadequate to cover the guilt
And all the while He strolls
  the gardens of our lives
  where we have lit the flames
  of our own hell here and now
Listen! A mellifluous voice:
  I am here

'Feel the soothing!' the cooling canopy
  of green leaves from His strength
'Look up!' the ceaseless cerulean
  skies of His caring
'Dive down!' the unfathomable
  depths of Her Love
The fire is quenched
There is no hell
  but ours to tell
  which God dispels

Dancing is Divine

In some quarters of our religious tradition
Dancing is of the devil and simply verboten
Seems to me they have never heard of, or maybe forgotten
The Dancing God
The God in Three Persons
  Who swirl
  Who swing
  Who spin
Who make way for the other but still remain three
  The Father
  The Son
  The Spirit
Who invite us to the happy harmony of the Great Dance
To wake up out of our earth-bound trance
Take as our partner the Triune God, and hold that stance
  We are His bride
  We are His joy
  We are His love
  His choosing
  His wooing
Making way for one another but still remaining me

The divine Dance is called *perichoresis*, which is Greek
All are invited to listen loudly for the music that we seek
We can all lean in and eagerly engage to take a peek
  At the invite
  With wonder
Gulping the grace
Linking hands with love
Dancing with the stars

Name Changes

God sees what we will become
So he meddles with our monikers
So history will show
   He is unfailingly true
So we will know
   His love fierce and unrelenting
   in the plans he has for us

While they were still barren and childless
   already old and quite unexpecting
By mere change or insertion of a letter or two
They became Abraham and Sarah, parents who grew
To be mother and father of countless generations

The terrorist called Saul,
   murderer of tender new believers
   'killing' Jesus at the same time
Now named Paul when he saw the light
   of the Love he was trying to obliterate

The tempestuous Cephas who
   flailed in the storm
The Lord he failed in the hour of need
   now declared his new appellation as Peter
   when he proclaimed Jesus the Living God

We are called members of God's family
   by His choosing and calling

And in some other sphere
  of time and space not clear
We'll be given a new name too

Will it be like our foreparents'?
A name that reflects who we are in His Eyes
  that defines us as we truly are
  amazing magnificent bright
  the pure and beloved
God's utter delight

Mishpocka*

Invite them all!
From every corner of the earth
Leave no one out

No color-coding of skin required
Shades now morph into one blinding brightness
No gender gaps with which to grapple
Now a family of equity, amity and sweet accord

Every 'other' is there
No more adherents of a lesser god
That prayer of long ago fully answered
All in union and synergy with God and one another

This is God's *mishpocka*
His blood-bought family called to celebrate oneness
Bound with ties whose tendrils trail the earth
And run deep root systems to connect all hearts

Not one is lost

*Yiddish, *extended family*

GRIEF AND LOSS

Three

Three trees
   their bare lacy branches
   silhouetted against cerulean sky
Three years
   since I walked this park
   with my forever-missed doggies
Today I breach the pain
   and take a solo stride

Such was the grip of grief

Three trees
Three years

When Loving Needs Comforting

When I think I can't continue to care
When it's just hurting too much
In the aching beauty of loving so deeply
I'm assured there is a place of plenty to touch, Yes!
The Source of my caring

I have touched the Divine
The Fountainhead
Real love that is limitless
Rips open the frail veil of the flesh
Devastates me
I mourn
I am comforted
I continue to free-fall into the endless supply

Stockpile of Sadness

They line up in the predawn
   sentinels of sadness
   clamoring for introspection
Their number is legion
Their shelf life bears
  no expiration date

Zerrissenheit*

A place of inner strife
Feeling torn to pieces on the inside
  Jagged shards of dissonance
  Jostling for the throne of disruption
This is not *gesundheit*
This is not health
This is sustained sickness of the soul
The antithesis of equilibrium of the whole

*German

Parting with Pets

They sicken and die
Part of our souls go with them
    never to be replaced
Their eyes appeal for release
    out of their silent pain
We do the hard thing—
We release them
But we don't know how to let go

We hold them for one last time
The vet is kind
Shortly after the shot
    the little chest no longer
    rises and falls
We have stopped a beating heart
The bark is silent
The bounding greeting gone
Wet nose no more

We don't know how we drove home
    to the empty house...

By-products of Bereavement

Crashing darkness in light of day
Insistent sleep
  occluding all conversation
A great weight. A great,
  heaving hopelessness
  blots out the sun at its zenith

This the trajectory of grief
  that I thought had fled
But even in the midst of
  all encompassing beauty
  of nature, my Montana cabin,
Out of everything comes nothing

As quickly as the shroud falls
It lifts like a switch
  inexplicable
  barely endurable
Grief has its own itinerary
  allowing no diversions

A Day Too Late

Full of expectation
Writing to let me know
Bursting with joy, hope and love
'I'll be looking for you
            Comin' in the voe.'*

I too in anticipation
Wanting to see you so
Eagerly tasting the welcome
Knowing you'd be looking for me
            Comin' in da voe

We didn't suspect the future
Couldn't preempt the blow
For only hope filled the time
Till you'd be looking for me
            Comin' in da voe

'Your father died this morning'
My heart cried, 'Say it's not so!'
Just one short day till my coming,
When I was looking forward to
            Comin' in da voe

The question faded unanswered
But one real truth is clear
Hope is replaced by sure faith
That you'll be looking for me
            Comin' over there

*da voe -Shetlandic, *the bay*

49

Wonder-Working Hope

The grip of grief has slackened its shackles
Hope, the thin, unbroken thread stretches
   to permit a spring in the step
Hope, the harbinger of happy
   highlights bright color and contrast
Though life is air brushed in sadness,
   though tears still wait willingly in the wings,
They serve now to baptize a reluctant convert
   into a new and different life
Hope springs eternal…

REGRET/FORGIVENESS

Blame and Shame…

They rhyme!
It is time
  to banish the pain
  to consider the gain
  of forgiveness and light
  where no shadow can blight
  radiant face held high
  no longer believing the lie

Evening Reverie

I scan the shifting sands
of my mind
and wonder
what I might find
to worry about tonight
at the close of a day
when all has gone right!

Happiness

What does it feel like?

Warmth finding its
way to the fingertips
tingling, transuding
all the way to the toes
before it goes
for it is fleeting

Disturbing the angst
at the confluence
of goodness and grace
like rivers in spate

An answered prayer
never too late
meets unexpected
kindness in a touch

Flowing head to toe
uniting the whole

And if it could last
fears would be past,
happy permanent

Forgiving

He was dying as he said
"Forgive them."

As I die to my pride
I too can say
'I forgive you.'

My Beloved's Absolution

He took my face in his gentle hands
  'You were the best caregiver
    anyone could ever have
  Remember that when guilt gnaws
    at the corners of your mind
  No guilt, none; I love you forever!'

Such is the gift he left behind
  to ease my troubled mind when
  remembering less than stellar days
  when fear and weariness won
    over grace

Who am I without this man of so many
  years by my side?
Some days are endless in their stretches
  of nothingness

No matter where I am
  there he is not—
How to find me without him?

But no guilt
Clean slate to start again ... sometime

This Christmas Day

Colored on the calendar of the ages
This Day demands cease-fire of all hostilities
The mind and the body are as still as night
Families and foes alike—though
They may be one and the same—come
Bearing gifts, offerings of peace and hope—
Tentative love

Time suspended
People from our always, absent but for this Day
Return to populate the celebrations
We capture their essence at table
Around the tree or making a toast
As logs crackle and crackers pop

A patina of bliss blends past and present
Erasing the regret of things not done
Easing the intrusive angst of tomorrow
Carols camouflage the dissonance
Just for this Day

The wars will resume in the morning

FAMILY

SHAMU (the Stuffed Toy) Went to The Zoo

Shamu went to the zoo one day
  with Triston his very best friend,
but Shamu got lost and left behind—
  Just how would this sad day end?

The zoo grew quiet, everyone went home,
  Triston cried cuz he'd lost Shamu,
but someone took him to the lost and found—
  Through the long, lonely night, *Boohoo!*

The animals heard little Shamu cry
  and came to make friends in the night.
Triston had prayed before he slept—
  All awaited the morning light.

Mommy phoned the zoo the very next day
  'Hello, Hello,' she said.
'Has anyone seen the Shamu we love?'—
  'Yes, he's here safe, warm and fed.'

Cries of delight and thanks to God—
  especially from Triston, his friend.
When Daddy and DanDan went to town that day
  they brought Shamu back—happy end!

Uno Alla Volta
One at a time

When they were small
  I took my children on
  a special date with Mama
  something of their choosing
  each child one at a time
As if each of them was the only one

One day at a time
  letting the present
  moment fill the screen
  aware and alert to its
  unrepeatable uniqueness
As if there were no past or future

One challenge at a time
  Listening in
  to the way forward
  A clear and focused
  mind to hear
As if there wasn't any confusion

One at a time
Our God listens
  as if each of us
  was the only one

My Brother

Music coursed through your veins
   the sea your milieu
   the island earth your grounding

To be ever free and unbound
   the drumbeat of your strong life
  brightest of stars in the far north skies

Now you are truly unfettered
   the universe your new domain
   playing endless riffs of riotous joy
   accompanied by glorious galaxies

Known at last as you always were known
   by your loving God
   His beloved child
   my brother

Child of The Isles

Bathed and birthed
in a womb of water
suspended
in solitude
distance and
distinction
a child of the different
of strength
out of deprivation
out of the water
wondering and
wandering
an unsteady youth
struggling to swim
where there is no water
with others who know nothing
of the distance
the difference
the distinction
a woman emerging from a
sea of solitude
takes her place in a world of many
bearing the wings of the water
the distance the distinct
forever a child of the isles

My Madeleine

The smell of a pipe evokes distant past
Tobacco smell brings back my father in a flash

His winsome wit
  his penetrating ponderings
  Reciting from memory long poems
  and Psalm 119, the longest psalm

His voice trembling
  tears filled his warm brown eyes
  as he told the story of Abraham and Isaac
  or cited grievous injustice among men

His tender hands
  let me paint a low wall in our house.
  My small, unskilled hands produced a mess
  but he did not repaint, change, or criticize

His strong arms
  embraced and held me without judgment
  (when I came to him as a young unwed mother)
  then later held his first-born granddaughter

The smell of a pipe is a madeleine
  memories of fragrance and presence
  and smoke curling upwards in the wind

Mother's Day Morning

A lass and a lady of far-flung Isles
Confined in body
   but not in mind
Your spirit ached and longed
   for wider horizons
Yet you blazed trails beyond your small world

You determined your daughter go where you never could

First in the community to discover a source
   for herbal medicine
   (how did you do that without Google!!?)
An untrained musician with a voice like a songbird
    whose self-taught scales on a little pump organ
    accompanied that voice and others who sang
     in the little island church

You determined your daughter go where you never could

You read everything that the tiny public library
   had to offer
You kept eloquent journals of your joys and sorrows
   your dreams and hopes
   your depression and loneliness
Through the separation of war and whaling expeditions
   that took my father far away for long months at a time

Your valiant heart lived to lose all but one sister of a
   family of seven

You determined your daughter go where you never could

Above all you taught me how to love
You loved me so well
   your unashamed Source, your Savior
You always wanted to see the orange groves
   of California
I have an orange tree in my Arizona backyard!
I proudly and humbly carry your invincible heart
   over continents and careers, to children
      and children's children

Your daughter did go where you longed to go

Your legacy is secure
Your DNA is safely deposited
   in the soil of great love
   in a fine family of hearts
   who continue to reach beyond the norms
   to color outside the lines

LIFE LENS

Creating a Cabin Retreat

The sounds of sanders, drills and saws
Creating concepts, ideas and dreams

Designers of hopes and happy homes
For people and music and art

Sounds of worship and joy
Sounds of work, which is praise

Sacred, all sacred—
Hammer and drill and plane

Long Time Online

Interminable waiting through monotonous music
Becoming less 'nice' with every note
Pressing a zillion numbers towards connection
Holding out hope of resolution
　　like peeling down through onion layers
...borderline tears of frustration

Finally hearing a real human voice...
　　sometimes hard to understand
　　too thickly accented
　　for ears now missing ranges of sounds
I say so ... they slow down

I let a smile break my surly disposition
The disembodied voice hears my smile

The music has ceased
No more numbers to push
There is just she and I now
We are the connection that matters
　　voice to voice, human to human
I make sure I know her name

'What's the weather in Seattle?'
'It's scorching hot in Phoenix!'

When I'm 'nice' a zillion good things happen!

They Have Their Reward

Lauding the great givers
  gives me the shivers.
What about the widow's mite,
  small but all, given out of sight?

How topsy-turvy is this world,
  not at all what we've been told
  by the One who knows
  and from Whom our bounty flows.

Goodbye at the Airport

Two little ones
  a boy and a girl
Saying goodbye to their daddy

The little girl spills over him
  copious unbridled grieving tears
Stock still, the boy shakes dad's hand
  staunching the lachrymal flow

Is the die so soon cast?

Girls become women who cry
Boys become men who don't

Rudeness on the Road

Well, he was driving an Audi after all
How could he wait
He might be late
For goodness sake
Small matter that he might take
  me out on the way to his urgent wake

No More 'Nice Day?'

Am I observing a deepening
of our casual encounters?

At the counter I'm bid adieu with
'Have a lovely day!'

The waitress returns the receipt with
'Have a wonderful day!'

Just a little shift now and again
A bit higher ground
I like the ascent!

Bickering and Blaming

Still in the headlines
   galvanized in their corners
   politicians posture and pout
No resolution

Blaming and bickering
   permeates walls and halls
   as pellets pierce hurting hearts
Nothing gets resolved

Blaming and bickering
   started in an idyllic Garden
   with mistrust, fear, shame
   the currency of our kind
So nothing gets resolved

Waiting Room Muse

Where I wait in the waiting room,
  magazines I rarely see abound.
I rub my wrist with perfume swatches.
Will anyone even notice I found
  a fragrance meant for men?
Will it matter?
What then!

Répondez s'il Vous Plait

I know it is French
   so sometimes I translate it into English
   on my invitations
Still that solicits not
   a glimmer of recognition or reply
I simmer with indignation
   stirring up a pot of resentment
   seasoned with not one charitable thought

I pull the pot off the boil
This pottage cannot cure bad manners

Voices of Vietnam

Are they mad?
Are they sad?
Are they glad?
I have no way of reading the intonations

The cadence is captivating
The pitch pronounced, vibrations varied
The utterly incomprehensible language
Dances up and down musical scales
    to my foreign ears
Monophthongs, diphthongs, and triphthongs
Sometimes talking all at once

Now I hear their wide laughter
They are not mad
They will pray in this tongue
They declare love in this tongue
They who left the land of this language
To become beautiful nails girls

Together at Thirty-Three Thousand Feet

Every conceivable shape and size
Some spill over narrow seats assigned—
   needing two slots maybe?
Many manage crying children...
   not very well!
Older and weaker needing help
Stunningly heavy 'hand carried' luggage
   defies their lift to the storage above
Most transfixed with electronics for the duration
Some read, still others snore throughout—
   how I envy them their sleep!
No food to anticipate, to punctuate the monotony
   nothing square and smelling savory
   wheeled softly down the aisle
Peanut packets do not assuage culinary craving
Plenty of drinks, thankfully, for many—
   too many maybe?
Conversations almost nil, are to be avoided—
   until we land
   Then it's deemed safe
   as it won't last long
And we can disembark as we boarded
Unknown companions who have endured a flight
Trapped together through another long night

Pillow Talk

Most pillows we have—
  some very old—
  have ominous label
  imbedded in the seam:

Do not Remove
under Penalty of Law

And we most certainly
  have vigilantly obeyed
  and utterly ignored the
  remainder of the order:

Except by Consumer

As we clutch in fear
  of a midnight hoist
  of pillows from beneath
  our sleepy heads

We tuck offending labels—
  as best we can—
  into pillowcases
  for the thousandth time,
  feeling safe and secure
  the whole night long
  from the long arm of the law!

America the Beautiful

Pilgrim from a more restricted place
to America, the parent
  of my progression
  land of my adoption.

Country of limitless opportunity
  for me and my progeny,
  ever grateful
  sometimes sad
  land divided
  in agony
  in greed
  in need
  of a re-birth of soul
  into a vibrant whole
  not of uniformity
  but of unity
  in our differences
  in our sameness
  with the world
  though still we hold
  that glorious space
  of being
  a framework
  of freedom.

Wide and wonderful land
  open your arms of welcome
  let us love one another

let us not fear one another
let us harness the love
and discover fire again.

Let us trade our hubris for humility,
  thee and me.

Poured Out or Sealed Up?

Shrink wrap confounds me
Those seals upon seals
   take the wind out of my sails
I want the cloistered contents contained therein
   and I want them now

I want to be on my way
   to sail forth on the waves of the day
   to pour out my uncontained exuberance
   to unload my unsealed supply of love and joy
On a waiting world wound around with wanting
   wanting to touch, to taste, to reach
   what they know is inside

Them, us, all the earth, the mystery once sealed
God wrapped in flesh, one of us
Now spilled over, poured out of the broken container
Walking on waves, unwinding the binding
   of the un-poured-out ones

THE JOURNEY

Desert Destination

From the wild open seas to the mountains,
    to round rolling hills and grand lakes ...
    the desert now claims my presence, takes
    my heart in this last gift of time ...
                    before the wakes.

Golden years like soaring saguaros, like
    communion coronets reaching for the sky,
    transcendent thoughts commune on high,
    join nature's praise of surrender and joy ...
                    until I can fly.

As wondrous wildflowers defy depiction
    drape barren mountains in spring,
    there where blossoms least expected to cling,
    from out of life's losses and longing ...
                    flowers still sing.

Perpetual sunshine, wrap around bliss
    of warm winter temperatures, soft and sweet,
    contrast to the desert held hostage to heat
    of summer from which there is no retreat ...
              ultimate metaphor for life itself.

The Darting Dots

One eye at a time focused on the stationary center dot
'Press the hand-held curser when you see a flash of light'
The more unsure of tracking accurately
The more I frantically press
With hope that my eyesight is not too diminished

The result shows I missed a lot
Lots of clumping dots in the periphery
Makes me think of friends and relationships
Some still brightly in focus
Others clumped in the corners of forgetfulness

Singers Without Voices

I have noted with growing wonder
on this journey of mine
how violence visits our lives-

Sickness strikes at the strongest points
   leaving its victim wounded,
   weakened, wondering,
   the handsome face
   devoured by cancer,
   the brilliant brain
   scrambled by stroke,
   the voice that sang like a lark
   silenced by Parkinson's ...

Singers all, silenced on the journey

Vain Voyager

I am astounded sometimes
  at my foolishness.
How can a woman of such vintage envy
  the flawless complexion of a twenty-something
  the still flat, firm belly of the forty year old
  the adroit, pain-free joints of her athlete grandchild?
But she does!
  then smiles ruefully in the looking glass at
  the sagging, slackening, stiffening, wrinkling
Older lass
And loves her

Carpe Diem

Living with designed intention
How swift are the seasons. The tension
of time and another dimension
Seizing the day
    not in hedonistic abandon
    but in humble plenitude
In this fleeting gift of time
    there is so much to unwrap
    before the bell tolls
Till it does, Carpe Diem is tattooed on my wrist
    and whispers to live in the moment first

Hiraeth*

I want to go back
  to what was
  before he died

I want to go back
  when my children were small
  before they grew up and went

I want to go back to my youth
  to vibrancy and beauty
  before I lost the bloom

I cannot go back to my Eden where
  a flaming sword stands at the gate

Turn around my sweet soul
  to what goodness still awaits

*Welsh (homesick for that to which you can never return;
  nostalgic grief for the lost past)

Children's Conclusions

*(In response to my protestations that I not be compared
to an old lady crossing the road in front of our car at
the stop sign)*

'Look! A grandma like you, Nanny!'
'What makes you say she's a grandmother?'
'Her hair is grey.'
'My hair isn't grey!'
   small pause …
'What color did it used to be?'

That was the day I decided to have a color rinse!

Again, from the back seat of the car, another grandson:
'Nanny, why don't grownups want to tell their age?'
'Ahh … because they don't want to be old.'
   Somewhat longer silence …
'Well, that's silly; they were young once,
   and all young people will be old one day;
   we all get our turn at all ages!'

That was the day I stopped being 'silly.'

And one more: On passing a daycare center
   after picking up a grandson from second grade:
   'Two things that should never be …. day care and war.'

That was the day I saw the child's eye view.

A Bit More Than Four

When you are neither a
  size two or a four
… but maybe a bit more,
Though the garment looks
  fetching on the model
… who is a two or four,
When it arrives in the mail
… in your bit larger size
  than the picture book,
'Tis not faintly amusing
  how different it looks
… on you who are larger
  than a two or four
… (though just a bit more
  than a two or four).

Oh, for goodness sake!

Longer and Slower

Things take longer when one is older
Maybe that's why we're made to slow down
Longer in the tooth is true too—
  one's gums recede
  spaces between teeth widen
Now brushing is not enough
  flossing no longer an option
  lest last night's spinach salad
  is on display at breakfast
  when you greet the new morning
  with a smile
  looking forward to a long, slow day

Things take longer when one is older
Yet … we have less time!

From Light To Light

Light flashes as sperm unites with egg
Divine ecstasy
Orgasmic delight
That an image bearer
Another to emanate light
Will burst upon this world
Brimming with promise and vigor and fight
For life and laughter and freedom
Without fear
While here
On planet earth
Until the race is over
   and the summons comes to return
   to throw off the cover
   that has dimmed the brightness of the promise
Again, the light
Just before they take flight

Love Second Time Around

A man called Ron
  ran a rapid deep root system
  into the ground of my being and
A tree of bright life has sprouted

Kindness and caring are the leaves
  that cover me
Through his strength I am released
  to see and feel again
I am beyond grateful
  outdistanced in delight
  overwhelmed with joy

Even though our leaves are falling
  in bursts of brilliance
The heart is forever young
Love and its attendant lightness
  lusciousness and warm desire
  know no chronology

So till the leaves are gone
  leaving but a skeleton of branches
  that reaches out to the promise
  of perpetual seasons
We will dance as the leaves fall,
  knowing there is forever
  in another form

RENEWAL

Maranatha

Come, Lord Jesus
Come to where you are
Remind me
Awaken me
  as I pull the empty pots in the burning heat
  the searing, scorching self-effort…
My well is dry

Come, Lord Jesus
Come to where you are
Let me hear the bubbling spring
  of supply from within
  that slakes thirst of longing
  that cools searing shame
  brings relief to the fearing

Come, Lord Jesus
  at the peak of the heat
  at the depth of the weakness
Speak of the promise again

Come…to where you always are

Dunamis

Some mornings I awake with a roar
  all my engines revving
  with the divine dunamis…
  I am ready to soar
When these days dawn
  dragons better hide
  for all will be slayed
  no stone left unturned
  every project done and dusted
With heart and mind one pulsing energy field
  no obstacle can hinder
  no person render me mute, inept
I will keep pace with the divine motor
All who come into this power field
  will know my energy signature

Some nights I fall into bed exhausted
Is such a pace and power a chimera?
  or merely the pot of clay
  that can't hold the sustained supernatural?
Frail and full of foibles,
  the dynamic energy of God
  is stilled while I sleep,
  the fragile container refreshed
  there at the dawn of a new day
  ready again for the fray

Pausing In the Passing Places

Our Way is called a Narrow Way
  often a lonely road
  a road of trusting uncertainty

I need
A passing place today
  like on remote Scottish highland roads
A place to wait as a truck trundles past
  till a slow moving flock of sheep clear
  the road and spill out onto the moor

I need
A safe space—no matter how small—
  to get off the road till my vision is clear
  till I can see through the tears
  till hands steady against the fears

I need
To simply stop there a while
  and smell the fragrant surroundings
  till the roar of accusation is dimmed
  till tragedy's torment is tamed

I need
To remember that my life
  is hidden in the cleft of the Rock
  that to surrender is to stay, to still,
  to remember love always makes a Way

I know
That this too shall pass

Feet Watching

On a long layover in Montreal airport
I settle down to contemplate
   the many feet passing by
Big ones, small ones
Limping ones, sprinting ones
New shoes, old sneaks
High heels, falling-apart flats
Army boots, brogans

Feet that are hurting
Some have walked miles
   walked away
   walked to
They all need washing
   to be held
   by tender hands
   in warm water

The water of life makes them clean
Only the feet need refreshing

Fig Tree Fulmination

Jesus cursing, not blessing?
He wanted food and it had no fruit
He could not simply be angry
　and impatient in his hunger
For petulant and presumptuous
　he was never
From the apocalyptic seedbed
　thinking of the time
Famine was real, something feared,
　but it was hoped
That Messiah would come,
　bring an end to hunger
And destroy the Devil's damning
　so no longer would starvation
　be a part of the world
That day the fig tree stood in the Way.
Messiah spoke the word that showed
　the back of the Curse
　was broken
He had the power to reverse the Fall,
　to curse the Curse,
The Kingdom was coming
　had come in Jesus
　has come in us

AMY WHITEHOUSE

ACKNOWLEDGMENTS

I may be from a faraway, isolated little Scottish island, but I am not an island in and of myself. This book of poems will testify to the need for the constant love and involvement of others for a productive life.

I thank my daughter, Sandra, for being the first to carefully read the manuscript and my many friends for their excitement and enthusiasm.

I am so grateful for my great, loving husband, Ron, and his love for—and affirmation of—my work.

I am humbly grateful for my editor Cathy Lawton, for her encouragement to write and submit these poems; for her wise and firm, though gentle, direction to make it the very best book possible.

And lastly, I am honored to host the exquisite artwork of my friend Amy, which both enhances and elevates the prose. This collaboration of pen and paint has been a joyous journey, and the final product delights us both.

Most of all, I acknowledge the God-given gift within me and the gift of living long enough to experience joy, pain and perspective—the rich soil of life from which these poems grew.

Alice Scott-Ferguson, a Scottish-born freelance writer and motivational speaker, was educated as a registered nurse in Scotland, holds a B.S. in Health Sciences, and has worked mainly in the psychiatric field.

She has contributed to both the secular and religious press and has authored several Bible studies.

An engaging and enthusiastic speaker, Alice has traveled internationally, presenting at various venues—women's seminars, writers workshops, and conferences for both women and men. She is passionately committed to bring God's liberating love and freedom to her audience.

In addition to Alice's collection of poetry, *Pausing in the Passing Places,* she has authored *Mothers Can't Be Everywhere, but God Is: A Liberating Look at Motherhood* (Cladach, 2002, 2018).

Earlier, she published *Little Women, Big God* (Essence, 1999), the story of the women's ministry she founded and directed in the U.K.

Alice co-authored, with Nancy Parker Brummett, *Reconcilable Differences: Two Friends Debate God's Role for Women* (David C. Cook, 2006)

Alice was widowed a few years ago and has recently remarried. Her family has now extended to include four step children and nine step grandchildren in addition to her own three natural children and six grandchildren who are scattered across the country.

Alice and her husband, Ron, live in Phoenix, Arizona.

She continues to lead several Bible study classes each week locally. Her passion is ever to teach and live out the fierce, limitless love of God.

9 781945 099083